My Little One's Book On "Habitats are Everywhere"

Alwina Kindo

Dedicated to

My Husband and Four precious gems Aakash, Adithya, Abishek and
Sparsha. You make me so proud. Always be the best you can be.
-Mommy

Book Info

This book is aligned with the national curriculum standards of science. This
book introduces the concept of Habitats and consider different habitats
from the farm to tundra and grasslands. They begin to understand the
importance of both living and nonliving in a habitat.
And how they interact with each other to stay alive. The images, repetition
of words and phrases support early readers and help the early readers to
understand the text. This book introduces early readers to subject - specific
vocabulary words which are defined in the glossary section. Toddlers or
some early readers may need some assistance to read some of the words.

Copyright @ 2020 by Alwina Kindo

This Book Belongs to

Date

Sprasha's Winter Trip to Look for a Home!

It was almost winter, The leaves were falling from the trees after turning brown.

The wind was whooshing by! Sparsha the Northern Pintail started to feel cold.

She knew the time has come for her to take her trip to the south.

The Northern Pintail flew towards her warmer home in times like this.

When the Northern Pintail flew to the hills and mountains,
Sparsha flew low to the ground to say "Hi!" to her friend the
mountain bear

She was tired so she landed on a pine tree to take a break and have some rest.

Sparsha noticed a mountain lion playing with her babies the cubs far below on the ground.

The Lion and the Lioness had a huge thick paws they were long and lean

This place was too cold for her to call it her winter home, so Sparsha decided to continue her journey.

The Northern Pintail came to a hot, dry desert. At first Sprasha did not see any animals or birds just sand and sand everywhere

When she flew low to snack on some dry seeds near a small shrub

She came face to face with a scorpion. The scorpion's skin was brown, just like the sand. When the scorpion stood still Sparsha couldn't see him at all

When Sparsha took off again she was startled at a jackrabbit. He hopped quickly across the sand kicking up clouds of dust with his tiny feet.

Sparsha could not find water anywhere. The deseret was not a good **habitat** for a Northern Pintail.

Northern Pintail now came close to the coast, where the sea meets the land.

As Sparsha flew over the ocean, she saw a group dolphins playing and leaping through the waves.

She saw other school of fish, she had no place to land. She said I can't stay here there is no room for me to make a soft warm nest

After a long exhausting trip, Sparsha and her other Northern Pintail friends reached their destination California.

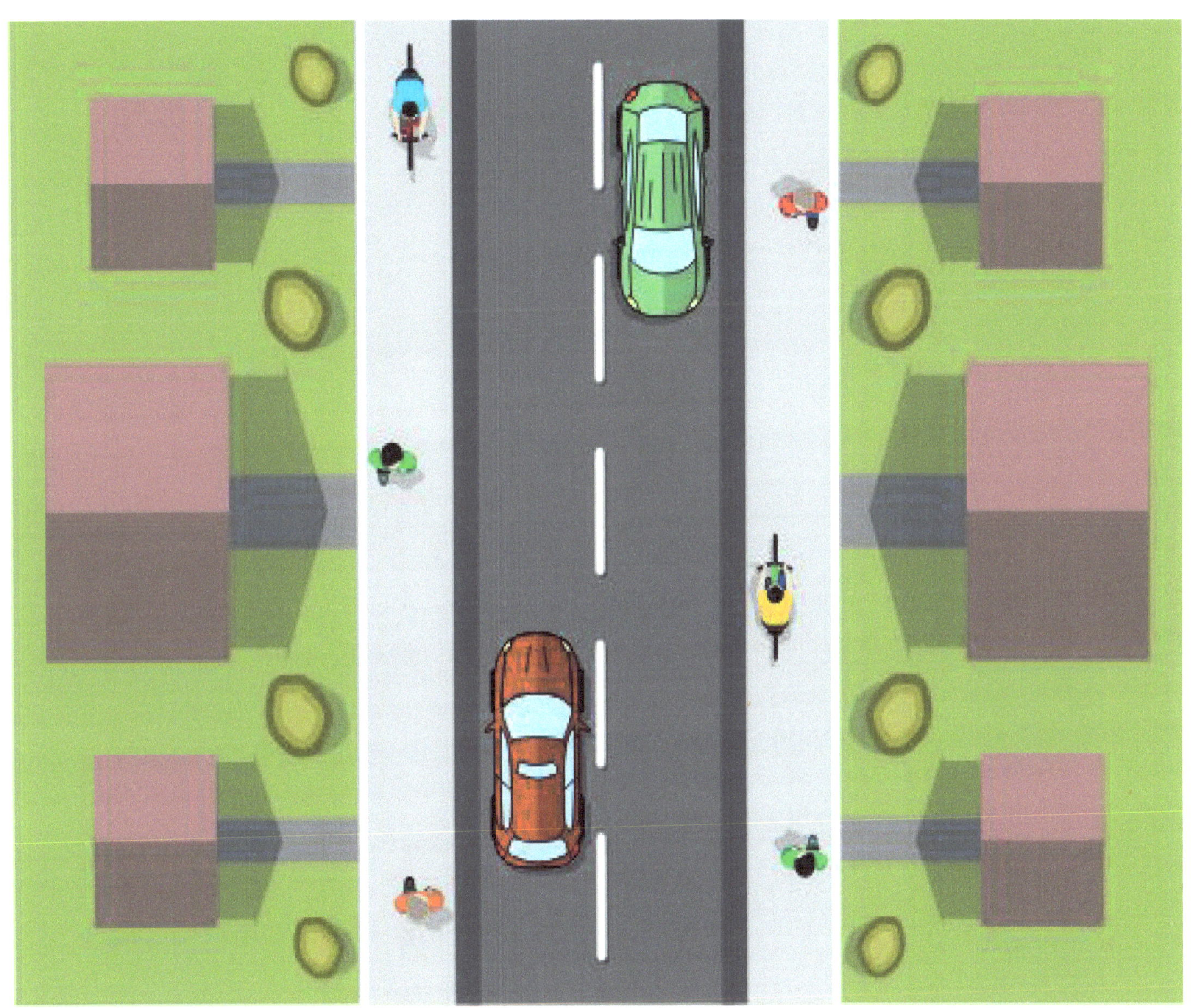

Sparsha watched the people pass by on the streets below and she heard loud honking of cars and trucks.

Sparsha found a nice wetland near the rice fields away from the city to make her winter home. A perfect time to spend daytime on the wetlands and feast on rice at night time

Sparsha found her habitat.

Life Science
Nonfiction
A Habitat Is a natural Home

Habitats can be seen on land, water or even in the air!

The place where the animals and plant live is called habitat

Plants and Animals need their own habitat to live or survive!

Plants and Animals have special characteristics to help them survive in a particular habitat

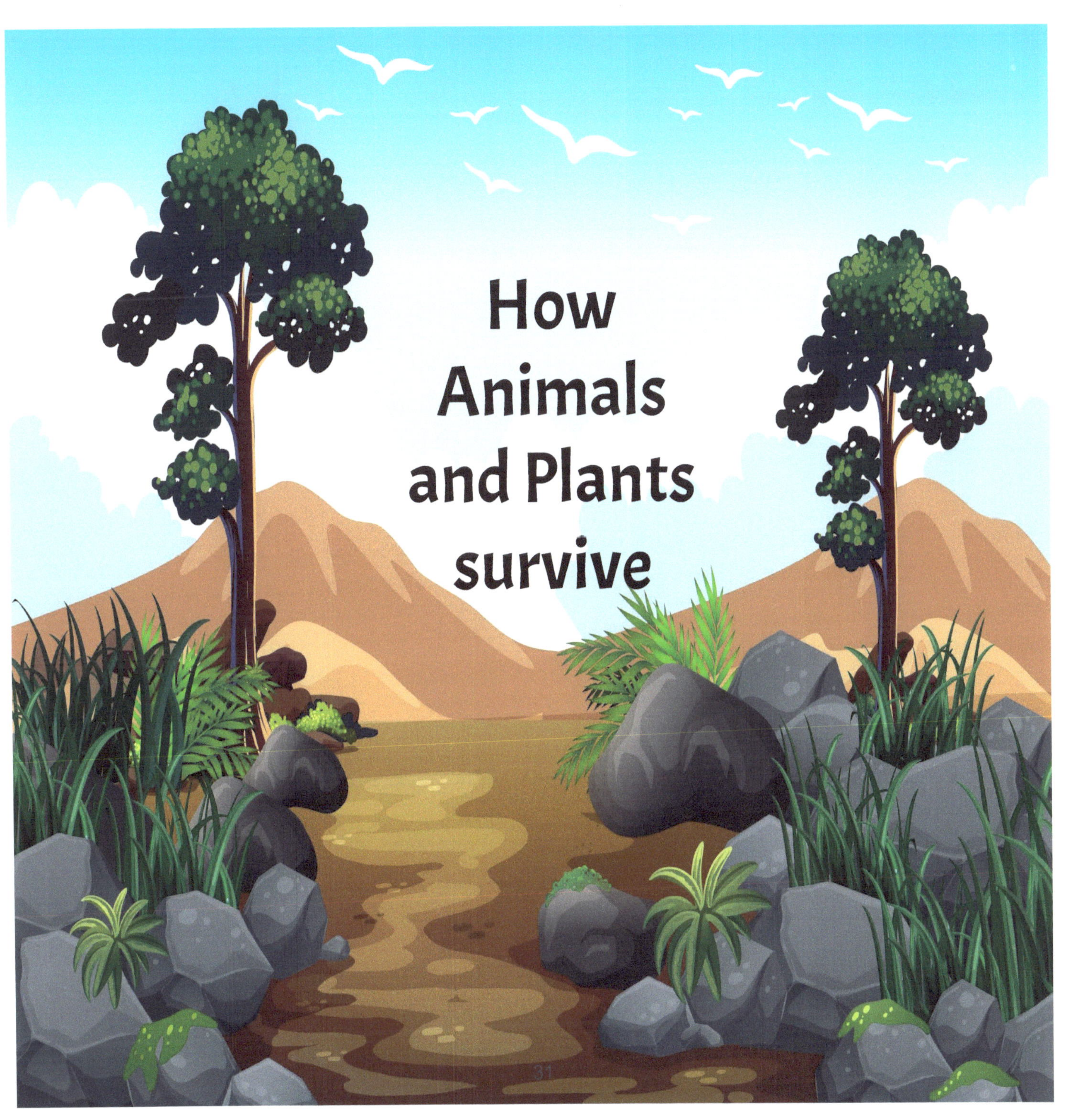

How
Animals
and Plants
survive

Deserts- It's extremely hot and very dry, still animals and plants live there.

Cactus in the desert can store water inside their stems so they can survive many days and months without rain.

Animals and Plants look different from places because of their habitat and **environment.**

Foxes who live in the forest look way different from foxes that live in snow and foxes that live in the desert habitat.

The fox fur helps the fox to blend in the habitat to prey on their food or to escape from their predators

Animals
and Plants
depend on
each other

Animals and plants rely on each other for many things.

Some animals need plants for food to get energy for their bodies

Some animals need plants for shelter to protect them from rain sunshine and predators.

Plants need animals to help them produce new plants for pollination

Forest is a perfect example for animals and plants living together and helping each other

Food Chain

Food Chain Concept

The food chain is how nutrients and energy are passed from creature to creature.

Ocean is very deep with salty water in it. Whales live in the ocean

Ocean is very deep with salty water in it. Whales live in the ocean.
Whales eat krill and krill eats phytoplankton

Predators eat other animals

Prey are animals that are hunted for food.

Activity

Which is the right answer

1. Which habitat is in the water?
a. Plains
b. Desert
c. Mountain
d. Oceans

2. What is the animal called that hunts other animals
a. A Habitat
b. A Prey
c. A Predator

3. What consists of a food chain?
a. Only animals
b. Only plants
c. Both animals and plants

4. Which animal is a prey to a tiger?
a. A Deer
b. A Whale
c. A Butterfly

Answers:-1. Oceans   2. A Predator   3. Both animals and plants 4. A Deer

Glossary

Desert:- A large, dry, sandy region,

Mountains:- A large big huge hill.

Habitat:- Environment where animals and plants live

Forest:- A big place filled with animals trees and plants

Food chain:- Where animals and plants depend on each other for energy

Ocean:- a very large expanse of sea,

Predator:- an animal that naturally preys on others for food to get its energy

Prey:- an animal that is hunted and killed by another for food.

Hope you enjoyed reading this
book.
Check out my other books

My Little One's Book On Learning All About Plants

My Little One's Book Of Living And Nonliving Things